Land of Liberty

Washington, D.C.

by Jason Glaser

Consultant:
Mychalene Giampaoli
Curator of Education
The Historical Society of
Washington, D.C. and
the City Museum

Capstone press
Mankato, Minnesota

Capstone Press

151 Good Counsel Drive • P.O. Box 669 • Mankato, Minnesota 56002

http://www.capstone-press.com

Copyright © 2004 by Capstone Press. All rights reserved.

No part of this publication may be reproduced in whole or in part, or stored in a retrieval system, or transmitted in any form or by any means, electronic, mechanical, photocopying, recording, or otherwise, without written permission of the publisher.

For information regarding permission, write to Capstone Press, 151 Good Counsel Drive, P.O. Box 669, Dept. R, Mankato, Minnesota 56002.

Printed in the United States of America

Library of Congress Cataloging-in-Publication Data
Glaser, Jason.
  Washington, D.C. / by Jason Glaser.
  v. cm.—(Land of liberty)
  Includes bibliographical references (p. 61) and index.
  Contents: About Washington, D.C.—Land, climate, and wildlife—History of Washington, D.C.—Government and politics—Economy and resources—People and culture—Recipe: cherry-chocolate ice cream—Washington, D.C.'s flag and seal.
  ISBN 0-7368-2204-6 (hardcover)
  1. Washington (D.C.)—Juvenile literature. [1. Washington (D.C.)] I. Title. II. Series.
F194.3.G58 2004
975.3—dc21   2002155471

Summary: An introduction to the geography, history, government, politics, economy, resources, people, and culture of Washington, D.C., including maps, charts, and a recipe.

Editorial Credits
Christopher Harbo, editor; Jennifer Schonborn, series designer; Molly Nei, book designer; Enoch Peterson, illustrator; Kelly Garvin, photo researcher; Eric Kudalis, product planning editor

Photo Credits
Cover images: Washington Monument, Digital Stock; Cherry blossoms, Corbis/Karen Tweedy-Holmes

Ann & Rob Simpson, 56; Anthony Mercieca/Photophile, 14; Brand X Pictures, 57; Bruce Coleman Inc./John Elk III, 44; Capstone Press/Gary Sundermeyer, 54; Corbis/Medford Historical Society Collection, 27; Corbis/Shepard Sherbell, 41; Courtesy of DC Vote, 37; Digital Stock, 1; Folio Inc./Richard T. Nowitz, 32, 63; Folio Inc./Rob Crandall, 8, 46; Getty Images/Alex Wong, 36; Getty Images/Hulton Archive, 24, 30–31, 49; Houserstock/Dave G. Houser, 12–13; Library of Congress, 18, 21, 58; Mae Scanlan, 17; One Mile Up Inc., 55 (both); Photri-Microstock, 25; Photri-Microstock/Richard T. Nowitz, 15; Photo by Carol Diehl, 50, 51, 52–53; PhotoDisc Inc., 38; Richard Cummins, 4, 42–43; Stock Montage Inc., 28; SuperStock, 22

Artistic Effects
Corbis, Digital Stock, PhotoDisc Inc.

The author dedicates this book to his father, Dallas Glaser, for his work in education.

1 2 3 4 5 6 08 07 06 05 04 03

Table of Contents

Chapter 1	About Washington, D.C.	5
Chapter 2	Land, Climate, and Wildlife	9
Chapter 3	History of Washington, D.C.	19
Chapter 4	Government and Politics	33
Chapter 5	Economy and Resources	39
Chapter 6	People and Culture	45

Maps
Washington, D.C. Sites 7
Washington, D.C.'s Land Features 11

Features
Recipe: Cherry-Chocolate Ice Cream 54
Washington, D.C.'s Flag and Seal 55
Almanac 56
Timeline 58
Words to Know 60
To Learn More 61
Internet Sites 61
Places to Write and Visit 62
Index 64

The large statue of Abraham Lincoln inside the Lincoln Memorial is 19 feet (5.8 meters) tall.

Chapter 1

About Washington, D.C.

Abraham Lincoln is considered one of the greatest U.S. presidents. He helped bring the Union and Confederate states back together after the Civil War (1861–1865). He also wrote the Emancipation Proclamation to free African Americans from slavery. On April 14, 1865, Lincoln was shot and killed at Ford's Theater in Washington, D.C.

One of the most popular tourist attractions in Washington is the memorial built in Lincoln's honor. The Lincoln Memorial reflects Lincoln's presidency. Thirty-six columns surround the outside of the building. They stand for the 36 states at the time of the Civil War. A giant statue of Lincoln sits in the center of the memorial. The words from

Did you know...?
The Lincoln Memorial is the building shown on the back of a penny. A tiny Lincoln statue is engraved in the center of the building. The statue can be seen with a magnifying glass.

Lincoln's Gettysburg Address and his second inaugural speech are written on the wall near the statue.

Workers began building the Lincoln Memorial in 1914. It was finished in 1922. The memorial is located at the end of the National Mall. It faces the U.S. Capitol and the Washington Monument.

The Nation's Capital

The District of Columbia is the home of the U.S. government. Federal government members and officials, including the president, live and work there.

The District of Columbia was made up of three cities when it was built. Washington City, Georgetown, and Alexandria were all inside the district's borders. Over time, Washington City grew and grew. The three cities grew into one large city. Now, all of the District of Columbia is called Washington, D.C. The district is not part of any state. The federal government and an elected city council run the city.

The District of Columbia lies along the Potomac River. Maryland borders it on the north, east, and south. Virginia lies

Washington, D.C. Sites

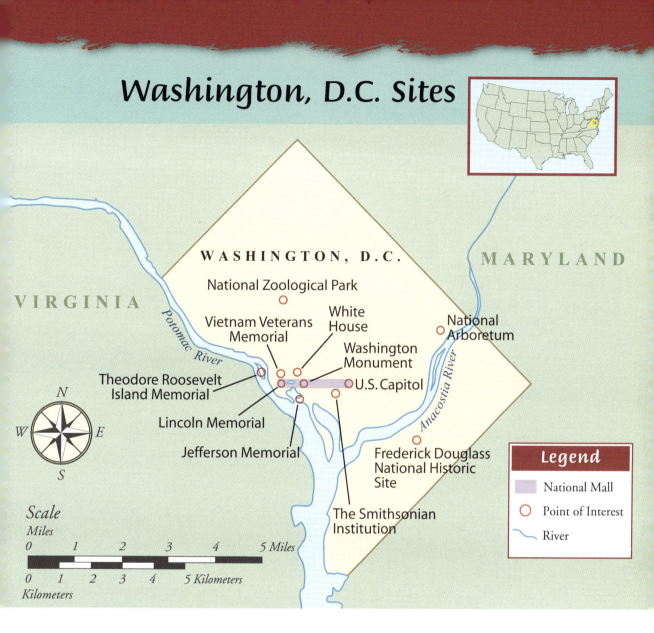

to the south and west across the Potomac River. More than 500,000 people live in Washington year-round. Thousands more live in the city part of the year while Congress is in session.

The Washington Monument rises more than 555 feet (169 meters) above the buildings and trees in Washington, D.C.

8

Chapter 2

Land, Climate, and Wildlife

Washington, D.C., was built on the marshlands and plains around the Potomac River. Very little remains of those marshlands today. Most of Washington's plants, trees, and animals are found in parks and areas around the Potomac.

Land Areas

The eastern half of Washington, D.C., lies on the Atlantic Coastal Plain. This area runs along the eastern and southern coasts of the United States. The Atlantic Coastal Plain starts near New York and New Jersey. It extends south into Mexico.

"[Washington, D.C.,] is the crossroads of the world."

—Pope John Paul II

Washington and other cities along the Atlantic Coastal Plain are very close to sea level. Some areas along the Potomac are only about 12 inches (30 centimeters) above sea level. The low areas are broken up by small hills. These hills rise less than 100 feet (30 meters) above sea level.

The western edge of Washington, D.C., lies along the Piedmont Plateau. This area runs along the base of the Appalachian Mountains. The term piedmont means the foot of the mountain.

The Piedmont Plateau and Atlantic Coastal Plain are separated by a fall line. A fall line forms when water flows from a region with hard rock into a region with softer rock. The water wears away the softer rock faster than the hard rock. The fall line creates rapids or waterfalls. The Potomac River passes through the fall line on its way into Washington.

Many Washington streets and buildings were built with rock from both the Piedmont Plateau and the Atlantic Coastal Plain. The Piedmont Plateau is filled with hard rock formed

Washington, D.C.'s Land Features

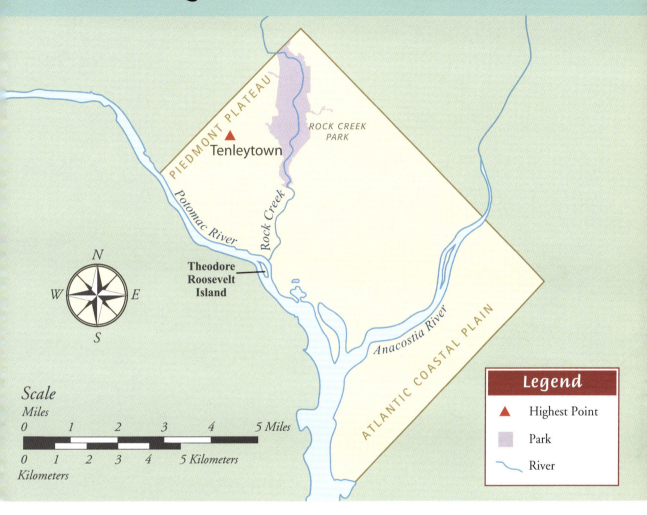

from old volcanoes. Granite mined from the Potomac River was used to build the U.S. Capitol's foundation. The Atlantic Coastal Plain has softer rock. This rock formed from soil flowing down rivers toward the ocean. Sandstone was mined from the Acquia Creek in Virginia. It was used to build the walls of the U.S. Capitol.

The Potomac River

The Potomac River begins as a small stream in West Virginia. It flows to the Atlantic Ocean. The section of the river near Washington, D.C., is part of the Potomac Basin. Water flows into the basin from the Potomac River, the Anacostia River, and other small rivers. In Washington's early days, these rivers fed many marshes and wetlands.

The Potomac River supplies about 75 percent of the city's drinking water. An average of about 7 billion gallons (26 billion liters) of water flow past Washington, D.C., each day. The city draws more than 460 million gallons (1.7 billion liters) of water a day for its residents. The Potomac is fairly clean because it is made up of melting snow and fresh rain. The city uses water treatment plants to purify the water. The treatment plants make it safe to drink

Melting snow and heavy rain can lead to flooding in Washington, D.C. In 1936, a heavy winter snowfall melted in

Sailboats travel up and down the Potomac River near Washington, D.C.

13

Great Blue Herons

The great blue heron is one of the most common birds in Washington, D.C. Great blue herons stand about 4 feet (1.2 meters) tall. They can have 6-foot (1.8-meter) wingspans. Their nests usually are built like platforms made from sticks. Some great blue herons nest alone, but most nest in colonies. They eat fish, plants, rodents, lizards, and turtles in or near the Potomac River.

Great blue herons are often found on Theodore Roosevelt Island. They also live in the trees along the Potomac River. Washington protects the tree line near the Potomac River and Rock Creek. The city also treats sewage that goes into the Potomac River. The treated sewage does not harm the plants and animals the herons eat.

a short period of time. The melting snow mixed with heavy March rains. The Potomac River rose more than 19 feet (6 meters) above flood stage. Areas of the city near the Potomac flooded.

Rock Creek Park

Rock Creek Park is one of the most beautiful nature spots in Washington, D.C. The park is 2,100 acres (850 hectares) in size. It begins at the northwestern border with Maryland. The park runs 15 miles (24 kilometers) down to the Kennedy Center. Rock Creek Park hosts historic sites such as Peirce Mill.

People enjoy visiting Peirce Falls at Rock Creek Park.

Did you know...?
A 17-foot (5.2-meter) statue of Theodore Roosevelt stands in the center of Theodore Roosevelt Island. The statue is surrounded by woods and can only be seen by hiking the island's trails.

This grain mill operated from 1820 to 1897. The National Park Service has opened a museum inside the mill. Rock Creek Park is also a popular spot for outdoor activities. People enjoy hiking, biking, picnicking, bird watching, and jogging at the park.

Theodore Roosevelt Island

Theodore Roosevelt Island is an 88-acre (36-hectare) island in the Potomac River. Many plants and animals live on the island. Ash, maple, oak, and elm trees grow there. Pawpaw and spicebush also grow on the island. Many rabbits, squirrels, turtles, and opossums make their homes on Theodore Roosevelt Island. Mallards, woodpeckers, cardinals, and great blue herons live on the island's shore and in the trees near the river.

Climate

The climate in Washington, D.C., is usually pleasant. Summers are warm. Winters are usually mild. The average winter temperature is 34 degrees Fahrenheit (1 degree Celsius). The average summer temperature is 74 degrees Fahrenheit (23 degrees Celsius). The Atlantic Ocean keeps the air in the city humid during the summer. During winter, freezing temperatures can turn rain showers into ice storms. Tropical storms along the Atlantic coast bring winds, rain, and snowfall. Washington gets about 41 inches (104 centimeters) of precipitation each year.

People visit the Lincoln Memorial during a snowstorm in March.

Fields and marshes surrounded Washington, D.C., in its early days.

Chapter 3

History of Washington, D.C.

The Nacostin, Anacostine, Susquehannok, and other Algonquin-speaking Indians were the first people to live in the Washington, D.C., area. They hunted and fished near their villages along the Potomac River for hundreds of years. They were living in the area when settlers arrived in the 1600s.

English settlers began arriving in Virginia in 1607. They built Jamestown along the James River. They started tobacco plantations in the new colony. In the 1620s, English leader George Calvert was given a section of Virginia near the Potomac River. Calvert's son, Leonard, led the first colonists into the area. He named the area Maryland.

"I see white buildings glistening in the sun. I see wide avenues and tree-lined parks. . . . I see the Capitol. This will be the home of Congress, the men who make the laws for our new nation."
—Pierre Charles L'Enfant, Washington, D.C., architect

A New Capital for a New Country

In the 1600s and early 1700s, England increased its power in the American colonies. England later became known as Great Britain. In 1754, the British fought for control of the colonies in the French and Indian War (1754–1763). This war drove the French out of the American colonies. After the war, the British began taxing common goods like paper and tea. Great Britain hoped to make back some of the money lost during the war.

British taxes led to the Revolutionary War (1775–1783). The colonists thought the taxes were unfair. In 1775, the people of Virginia, Maryland, and 11 other colonies demanded freedom from Britain. The colonies won their independence in 1783. The first capital of the new United States of America was set up in Philadelphia, Pennsylvania.

After George Washington was elected president in 1789, many other cities wanted to be the capital. Finally, Congress decided a new capital city needed to be built. The southern states and the northern states could not agree where to build the new capital. All the states believed that areas closest to the capital would have control over the new government.

The government wanted Congress, not a state, to control the new capital. A bill was passed allowing George Washington to choose the site for the new city. Washington wanted to build the capital city near his home in Virginia. In 1791, Washington chose a 10-square-mile (26-square-kilometer) area along the Potomac River. The new capital district was carved out of the states of Maryland and Virginia. The cities of Alexandria and Georgetown were inside the district's borders.

After George Washington picked a site, Pierre Charles L'Enfant drew a map of the city. His plans called for a grand capital city with long, wide streets.

George Washington studied Pierre Charles L'Enfant's plans during the building of the city.

Building the Capital

George Washington chose a French architect named Pierre Charles L'Enfant to design the District of Columbia. Washington also asked Andrew Ellicott and a free African American named Benjamin Banneker to help survey the area. Banneker was a farmer and a friend of Ellicott's.

L'Enfant wanted to build a grand capital city. His plans called for large, wide roads. These roads made wealthy landowners in the area angry. Landowners were paid for the land used in building the capital, but they were not paid for the land used for roads. Many landowners felt they were being cheated out of money because so much land was used for roads.

L'Enfant believed he could do whatever he wanted while building the city. He ordered workers to tear down a house because it was in the way of his plans. The owner of the house was a friend of George Washington. Washington and L'Enfant began having troubles working together. Washington fired L'Enfant after two years of work. Ellicott then became the chief designer of the city.

> **Did you know...?**
> Thomas Jefferson ran a contest in the newspaper to choose the architect for the President's House, later named the White House. The design by Irish immigrant James Hoban won the contest. Construction of the White House began in 1792.

The Government Moves In

After eight years in office, George Washington retired from the presidency. In 1799, he died at his home in Virginia. President John Adams and other politicians agreed to honor Washington

Dolley Madison

In the early 1800s, Dolley Madison was one of Washington, D.C.'s most popular people. As President James Madison's wife, Dolley loved fashion and wore exciting clothes. In the White House, Dolley hosted dinners and parties. She made her guests feel welcome. She hosted the first inaugural ball in 1809.

Without Dolley, many historical papers and works of art would not have survived the War of 1812 (1812–1814). When the British army invaded Washington, soldiers burned down the White House. Before leaving the city, Dolley saved many of the president's papers. She also saved a portrait of George Washington.

by moving to the new capital early. They also named the main city in the district Washington City.

Washington was still being built when President Adams and Congress came in 1800. The streets were not paved. The city was dusty in the summer. Streets were muddy in the winter. Washington had few houses. People had to live in boarding houses and hotels. Food was brought in from nearby farms and sold at Center Market.

The War of 1812

The War of 1812 between the United States and Great Britain almost destroyed Washington. In 1814, British troops attacked the city. They set fire to many buildings, including the Capitol and the President's House, later named the White House.

The British set fire to the President's House in 1814 during the War of 1812.

Did you know...?
During the Civil War, Fort Stevens helped protect Washington, D.C., from the Confederate Army. President Abraham Lincoln visited the fort during the Battle of Fort Stevens in 1864. It is the only time an active U.S. president has come under enemy fire during battle.

Many of the rooms in the President's House were scorched by fire. The whole building would have been completely destroyed had it not begun to rain.

The Civil War

From the time the capital was built, slavery and politics divided the country. Northern states believed using people as slaves was wrong. Southern states used slaves to plant and harvest crops. The southern states also believed that state government was more important than federal government.

After Abraham Lincoln's election in 1861, 11 southern states separated from the United States. They formed the Confederate States of America. The Civil War broke out between the North and the South.

Washington became an important location during the war. The city was near the edge of the Confederate states. President Lincoln called for troops and supplies to help defend the city.

In 1862, Lincoln abolished slavery in the city. Many slaves and former slaves came to Washington during and after the war.

Union officers stood near a cannon at Fort Gaines while protecting Washington, D.C., during the Civil War.

After the Civil War, slavery was abolished in the whole nation. Southern states gradually rejoined the union.

The Late 1800s

Washington grew rapidly during the 1860s and 1870s. Workers built new roads, canals, houses, and stores. In 1871,

Alexander "Boss" Shepherd was appointed to the Board of Public Works. He paved streets. He put in water and sewer lines. He worked hard to make Washington a better place to live.

In 1893, Congress passed a law to extend the city of Washington into the rest of the District of Columbia. Many tall buildings were built. In 1899, Congress passed a law that said no building could be taller than the Capitol dome. In 1910, the law was changed. No building could be built taller than the Washington Monument.

Trolleys carried people up and down the broad streets of Washington, D.C., in the late 1800s.

The 1900s

In the early 1900s, people from all over the country traveled to Washington, D.C. Many people came during times of national crisis. During World War I (1914–1918) and World War II (1939–1945), Americans traveled to the city to help with war efforts. Many people looked to Washington for information and support during wartime.

People also went to Washington when times were tough. In 1932, more than 20,000 World War I veterans came to Washington. They wanted "bonus pay" for time served in the war. They camped in the city's parks for several months. President Herbert Hoover had to order the army to move the veterans out of Washington, D.C.

In the 1950s and 1960s, African Americans across the country led marches and protests during their fight for equal rights. Washington's large African American population made the city a center for the Civil Rights movement. Washington became a common location for many large

> **Did you know...?**
> The Washington Monument was built in two stages. The first 151 feet (46 meters) of the monument were built between 1848 and 1858. The last 404 feet (123 meters) were built between 1878 and 1888.

protests and demonstrations. Martin Luther King Jr. gave his famous "I Have a Dream" speech at the Lincoln Memorial in 1963.

Recent Years

In recent years, national security has become an important issue in Washington, D.C. In 2001, Washington was threatened when hijackers captured four American airplanes.

Two planes were crashed into the World Trade Center in New York City. Another was flown into the Pentagon in the Washington, D.C., area. Many people believed that the fourth plane was being flown toward the White House. Passengers on the plane overpowered the hijackers. They caused the plane to crash in a Pennsylvania field before it could reach Washington. Since then, the government has increased security in the city to protect Washington's citizens and visitors.

On August 28, 1963, thousands of people gathered on the National Mall to hear Martin Luther King Jr. give his "I Have a Dream" speech on the steps of the Lincoln Memorial.

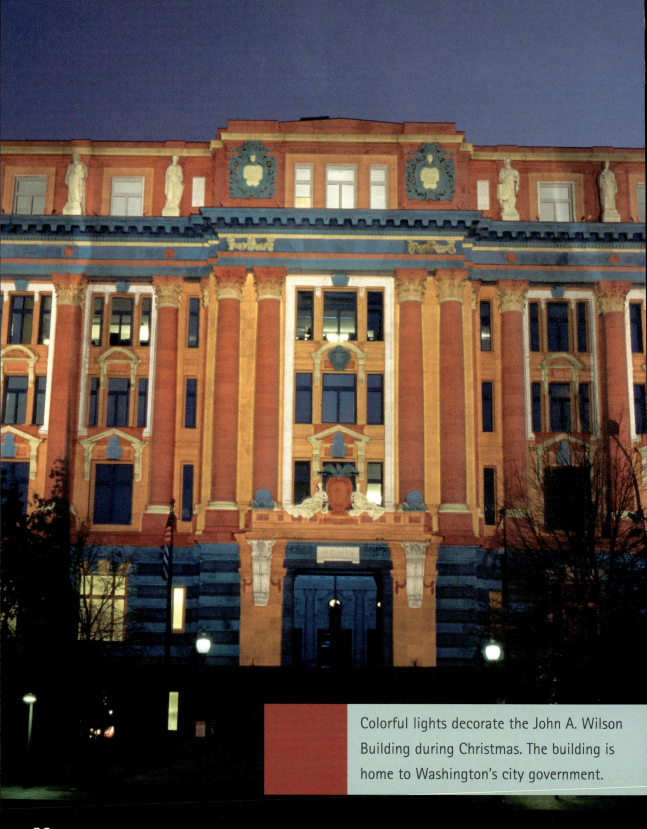

Colorful lights decorate the John A. Wilson Building during Christmas. The building is home to Washington's city government.

Chapter 4

Government and Politics

Washington, D.C., hosts the highest levels of government in the United States. The president, vice president, members of Congress, and Supreme Court justices work there. Their work affects the lives of everyone in the United States.

The people living in Washington live under a different form of government than other Americans. The city is not part of a state. The federal government controls many of the city's laws.

City Government

Washington, D.C., is run by a form of home rule. Congress controls part of the city's budget. The city can elect its own

"I was the nation's first black mayor of a major city, and that generated great excitement in the black community. But it was a tense time. There was the sense that a tiny spark could ignite the anger and the rage that people felt."
—Walter Washington, Washington, D.C., mayor, 1975–1978

leaders who make laws. Since 1975, the city has elected the mayor, city council members, and neighborhood advisors.

Like most states, Washington's city government has three main branches. The mayor leads the executive branch. The mayor plans the city budget. The mayor also chooses people to lead the city's fire and police departments.

The city council is Washington's legislative branch. The council approves the city's yearly budget. The council also writes new laws. The council has 13 members. Eight members are elected from the city's eight divisions, called wards. The other five council members are elected from the city at-large. This means they are elected without regard to the ward in which they live. The city also elects neighborhood advisors. These advisors bring neighborhood issues to the city council.

The District of Columbia Court of Appeals leads Washington's judicial branch. The court of appeals reviews cases appealed from the superior court. The Superior Court of Washington, D.C., is divided into civil, criminal, family,

Washington, D.C.'s Government

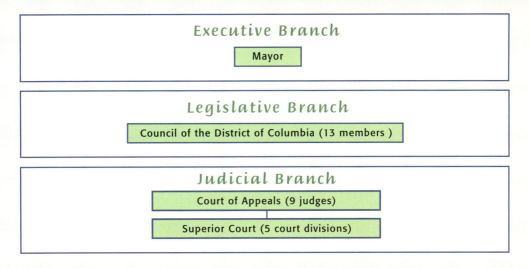

probate, and multi-door resolution courts. The multi-door resolution court hears a variety of cases, including child protection and tax cases.

Battle for Power

The U.S. Congress limits the power of Washington's home rule. In 1997, Congress created a control board to help the city's finances. The city was $500 million in debt. In 2001, the control board was dissolved after the district went several years without overspending.

Congress also decides what can be taxed in the district. Washington, D.C., is not allowed to collect property taxes on federal buildings. Federal buildings make up 53 percent of the buildings in Washington, D.C.

The city also cannot collect income tax from people who are part-time residents. More than 1 million people who live and work in Washington all year claim they live outside the district. Because of these tax laws, Washington often spends more to support the city than it can collect in taxes.

In January 2003, members of the U.S. House of Representatives were sworn into office. The representative for Washington, D.C., can sit in on committee meetings, but can not vote on legislation.

Burning the 1040s

U.S. citizens pay income taxes to the federal government each year. They fill out forms called 1040s. The forms are due by April 15. On April 16 every year, some citizens of Washington, D.C., burn copies of their 1040s in protests. They do this because they do not have a voting representative in Congress. They have no control over how their tax money is spent. The protesters chant, "Taxation without representation is tyranny!" This is the same protest raised during the time of the Boston Tea Party before the Revolutionary War.

Leaders of Washington, D.C., have passed bills many times to apply for statehood. As a state, Washington, D.C., could have representatives and senators like other states. Congress has defeated each of the bills for statehood.

Today, Washington, D.C., has three electoral votes in presidential elections and two elected members to Congress. One member serves in the House of Representatives. The other member serves in the Senate. The representative and the senator are not allowed to vote in Congress.

The U.S. Capitol's dome was built in the 1860s. The dome is made out of 8,909,200 pounds (4,041,213 kilograms) of cast iron.

Chapter 5

Economy and Resources

Washington, D.C., has a limited economy. The city is not large enough to support many of the industries that support other states. The city does not have farmland to grow crops. It has few manufacturing industries to make products. Washington's economy is based on government, service industries, and tourism.

The U.S. Government Workforce

Many people work for the U.S. government in Washington. All of the politicians in Washington have staff members who work for them. Senators, representatives, Supreme Court justices, and their staffs live in Washington many months out

Did you know...?
The White House employs five full-time chefs. They can prepare meals for dinner parties of up to 140 people.

of the year. The White House also has a large staff. Lawyers, policy advisors, speechwriters, secretaries, and personal assistants work at the White House. The federal government also pays workers in federal organizations. These organizations include the Internal Revenue Service and the Social Security Administration.

Thousands of lobbyists work in Washington, D.C. Many businesses and groups in the United States are interested in the laws Congress passes. Companies and organizations hire lobbyists to talk to politicians. Lobbyists try to get politicians to vote for laws that will help their companies or industries.

The U.S. military has many people working in Washington, D.C. The president of the United States is called the commander-in-chief. The commander-in-chief is in charge of the armed forces. The Joint Chiefs of Staff also work in Washington. This group of high-ranking military officers works with the president on military plans and national defense issues. Thousands of men and women in the military work at Bolling Air Force Base, Fort Lesley J. McNair, and the Washington Navy Yard.

Think Tanks

Think tanks are one of Washington's unique businesses. A think tank is a business that finds solutions to difficult problems. Some think tanks look at events happening in other countries. They study how those events will affect the U.S. economy or government.

The Heritage Foundation (at left) is one of the largest think tanks in Washington, D.C. It studies how foreign governments will react to American policies. The Heritage Foundation helps the U.S. government decide if it should take military action in other countries.

Service Industries and Tourism

Many businesses in Washington, D.C., provide services to the people working in the city. Washington has many large legal and accounting firms. These firms stay informed about new legal or economic changes. Congress sometimes hires these firms to help with government work.

Some areas in Washington, D.C., need a high amount of security. Washington hires many guards and police officers to protect historic and federal sites. A police motorcade guards the president and other important leaders as they travel in the city.

Other businesses support Washington's residents and visitors. World leaders and more than 19 million tourists visit the city each year. The city has many restaurants, hotels, museums, and stores. Washington hires bus drivers and taxi drivers. The city also hires workers to run the rail transit system.

Tourists visit many monuments, memorials, and historic sites in Washington, D.C. The U.S. Capitol, the Lincoln Memorial, the Washington Monument, and the Smithsonian Institution are located along a strip of land called the National Mall. Other popular sites include the Vietnam Veterans Memorial, the White House, the National Zoo, and the Supreme Court. People also visit Georgetown, Shaw, Dupont Circle, and other historic neighborhoods in the city.

The Smithsonian's oldest building is located along the National Mall. Called the Castle, it serves as an information center for the Institution's 14 national museums.

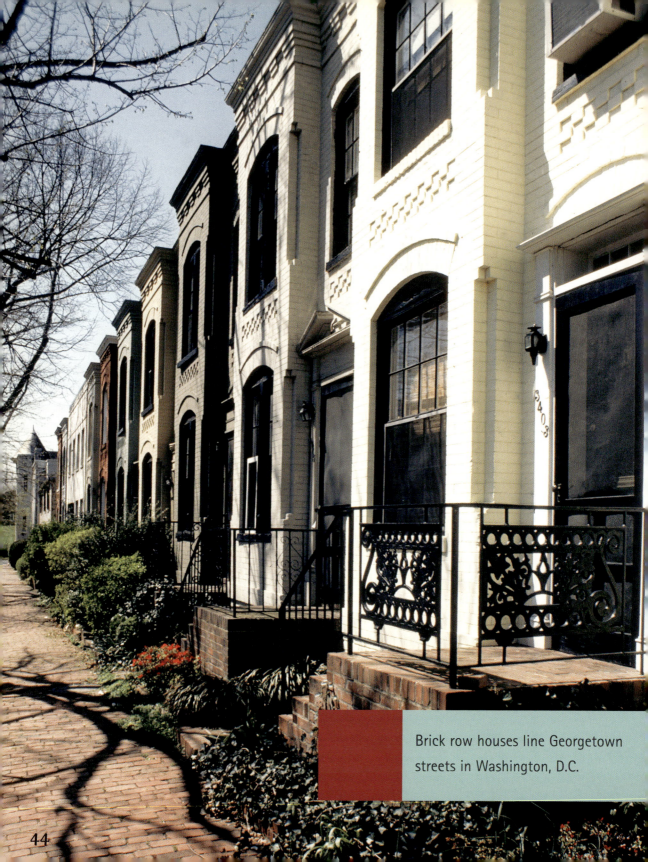

Brick row houses line Georgetown streets in Washington, D.C.

Chapter 6

People and Culture

Washington, D.C., was built to represent the people of the United States. The city reflects much of the nation's diversity. People of many races and cultures live in and visit the city. The city's buildings range from grand federal buildings to mansions, condominiums, row houses, and duplexes.

In recent years, Washington's population has increased. Crime rates have fallen. More and more people are moving to the city to buy homes, rent office space, and start businesses.

African American Population

Washington has always been a key city for developing African American culture and equality. Since its early days, Washington has had a large African American population. Today, about 60 percent of Washington's citizens are African American.

Martin Luther King Jr., Louis Farrakhan, and other African American leaders have traveled to Washington, D.C., for rallies. In 1995, Farrakhan and other African American leaders led the Million Man March. One goal of the march was to encourage African American men to improve relationships with their families. Thousands of African Americans traveled from across the country to take part in the march.

Thousands of people marched through the National Mall to the steps of the Capitol during the Million Man March in 1995.

Washington, D.C.'s Ethnic Backgrounds

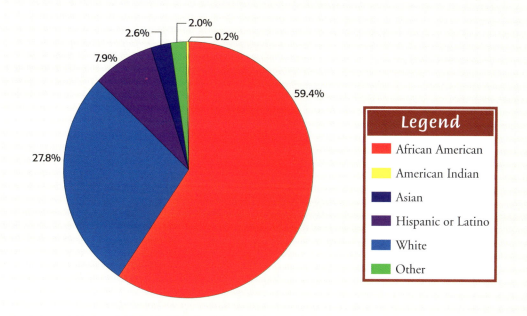

Washington, D.C., was also the home of Carter G. Woodson. Woodson has been called "the Father of Black History." He was among the first people to record and preserve African American achievements.

Music

Many people see Washington, D.C., as a city of jazz. Jazz music began in Louisiana and was heavily shaped by African

"When people want to learn about our rich African American history and heritage, they come to D.C. . . . where African Americans flocked to get a first rate education during the darkest days of segregation."
—Mayor Anthony A. Williams, 2002 State of the District Address

American musicians. Famous jazz musician Duke Ellington was born in Washington, D.C.

In the 1970s, Chuck Brown started a type of music in Washington, D.C., called "go-go." Go-go combines jazz, rhythm and blues, African beats, and religious call and response. While the music plays, musicians call out words and phrases and the audience responds.

Life in the City

Washington, D.C., neighborhoods are rich in culture and history. Many Latino Americans and Asian Americans live in the Mount Pleasant neighborhood. The Latin American Youth Center is in Mount Pleasant. Many Latino Americans also live in the Adams Morgan neighborhood. The Latino Community Heritage Center is in Adams Morgan. The center teaches people about the lives of Latino immigrants who settled in the Washington, D.C., area.

Georgetown is a historic neighborhood in Washington. The neighborhood has many old Victorian homes built by

Duke Ellington was one of the world's best jazz pianists. He was born in Washington, D.C., in 1899.

early landowners. Sometimes these homes are called brick row houses. They were modeled after homes built in England during the Victorian Era. The houses are tall, narrow, and built from bricks or cut stone. Georgetown celebrated its 250th birthday in 2002. Many brick row houses were used to reenact life in the 1700s.

Cherry Blossoms

In 1912, Japan gave several thousand cherry blossom trees to President William Howard Taft. Called "Sakura," the trees were symbols of an ongoing friendship between the United States and Japan. Two of the original trees are still alive today.

In 1999, Japan presented the United States with 50 more cherry blossom trees. These trees are descended from a 1,500-year-old tree growing in Japan. That tree is a Japanese National Treasure. People believe Emperor Keitai planted the tree after becoming emperor of Japan.

The Anacostia neighborhood also has a rich history. The home of abolitionist Frederick Douglass is in Anacostia. Douglass' home and the Anacostia Neighborhood Museum show some of the history of African American culture in Washington, D.C., and the United States.

Culture

Washington, D.C., is home to the National Arboretum and the Library of Congress. The National Arboretum has 446 acres (180 hectares) of gardens. It grows hundreds of plants that do not grow naturally in the United States. The Library of Congress is the largest library in the country. More than 120 million items are part of the library's collection.

Large lilypads grow at the National Arboretum.

The Smithsonian Institution is the largest museum in the nation. The Smithsonian began in 1829. Englishman James Smithson gave Congress 105 sacks of gold. Smithson wanted the money to be used to help share knowledge with people. Today, the Smithsonian's museums hold dinosaur fossils, NASA spacecraft, and famous works of art.

The John F. Kennedy Center for the Performing Arts presents more than 3,000 performances each year. The center has five theaters. Audiences can see the world's greatest

dancers, musicians, and other performers. The center opened in 1971. It has hosted operas, ballets, jazz concerts, and plays.

Washington, D.C., is more than just famous monuments and memorials. Neighborhoods, such as Georgetown and Anacostia, teach people about the city's past. Rock Creek Park and Theodore Roosevelt Island show people the nature within the nation's capital. From the Potomac River to the Smithsonian, Washington, D.C., has many places to visit and enjoy.

The John F. Kennedy Center for the Performing Arts sits on the banks of the Potomac River.

Cherry-Chocolate Ice Cream

Thomas Jefferson and Dolley Madison both enjoyed making ice cream when they lived in the White House. This homemade cherry-chocolate ice cream honors Washington's spring cherry blossoms.

Ingredients

1 pint (480 mL) half and half
½ cup (120 mL) sugar
1 teaspoon (5 mL) vanilla
¼ cup (60 mL) canned cherries, drained
¼ cup (60 mL) milk chocolate chunks
1 5-pound (2.25-kilogram) bag of small ice cubes
2 cups (480 mL) salt

Equipment

liquid measuring cup
dry-ingredient measuring cup
measuring spoons
1 small, clean coffee can with lid
1 large, clean coffee can with lid
wooden spoon
pot holders

What You Do

1. Put half and half, sugar, vanilla, cherries, and chocolate chunks in the small coffee can.
2. Stir the above ingredients together with a wooden spoon.
3. Place the lid tightly on the small can.
4. Put the small coffee can in the middle of the large coffee can.
5. Place ice around the small can. The ice should fill the large can.
6. Pour 1 cup (250 mL) of salt over the ice.
7. Seal the lid tightly on the large can.
8. Using pot holders, roll the can around on the floor for 10 minutes.
9. After 10 minutes, take the small can out of the large can. Have an adult help you remove the lid and stir the ice cream mixture with a wooden spoon.
10. Take the large can and pour out the ice and water into a sink.
11. Repeat steps 3 through 9.
12. Serve ice cream immediately or store ice cream in freezer.

Makes 4–6 servings

Washington, D.C.'s Flag and Seal

Washington, D.C.'s Flag

Washington, D.C., adopted the district flag in 1938. It shows three red stars and two red bars on a white field. The flag is based on the shield of George Washington's coat of arms.

Washington, D.C.'s Seal

Washington, D.C., adopted its official seal in 1871. The seal shows a woman placing a wreath on George Washington's statue. The woman represents justice. A bald eagle, the national bird, sits to next to the woman. The U.S. Capitol is seen behind her. A ribbon with the city's motto is at the bottom of the seal. "Justitia Omnibus" means "Justice for All" in Latin.

55

Almanac

General Facts

Nickname: The Nation's Capital

Population: 572,059 (U.S. Census 2000)

Geography

Area: 68 square miles (176 square kilometers)

Highest point: Tenleytown, 410 feet (125 meters) above sea level

Lowest point: Potomac River, 1 foot (.3 meter) above sea level

Famous Sites

Government buildings: The White House, U.S. Capitol, U.S. Supreme Court, U.S. Postal Service Headquarters

Historic sites: Ford's Theater, Jefferson Memorial, Korean War Memorial, Union Station, United States Holocaust Memorial

Climate

Average summer temperature: 74 degrees Fahrenheit (23 degrees Celsius)

Average winter temperature: 34 degrees Fahrenheit (1 degree Celsius)

Average annual precipitation: 41 inches (104 centimeters)

Wood thrush

American beauty rose

Symbols

Bird: Wood thrush

Flower: American beauty rose

Song: "Washington," by Jimmie Dodd

Tree: Scarlet oak

Economy

Types of industry: Government, tourism, service industries

Manufactured products: Newspapers, magazines

Sports Teams

MLS: D.C. United

NBA: Washington Wizards

NFL: Washington Redskins

NHL: Washington Capitals

WNBA: Washington Mystics

WUSA: Washington Freedom

Government

First elected mayor: Walter Washington, 1975–1979

Year became U.S. capital: 1800

U.S. Representatives: 1

U.S. Senators: 1

U.S. electoral votes: 3

Wards: 8

57

Timeline

Washington, D.C. History

1600s
Nacostin, Anacostine, and Susquehannok tribes live in Washington, D.C., area.

1620s
Leonard Calvert leads settlers into Maryland.

1791
George Washington selects the location for the capital.

1814
The President's House is burned by British troops.

1863
President Lincoln signs the Emancipation Proclamation to free African American slaves in the South.

1862
President Lincoln abolishes slavery in Washington, D.C.

U.S. History

1620
Pilgrims establish Massachusetts Bay Colony.

1775–1783
American colonies fight for independence from Great Britain in the Revolutionary War.

1812–1814
The United States fights Great Britain in the War of 1812.

1861–1865
Union states fight Confederate states in the Civil War.

1932
World War I veterans come to Washington, D.C., to protest for "bonus pay" for time served in the war.

1893
Congress passes a law extending the city of Washington into the rest of the District of Columbia.

1963
Martin Luther King Jr. makes his "I Have a Dream" speech in Washington.

1970s
Chuck Brown starts a type of music in Washington, D.C., called go-go.

1995
The Million Man March is held on the National Mall.

1929–1939
The United States experiences the Great Depression.

1964
U.S. Congress passes the Civil Rights Act, making discrimination illegal.

1914–1918
World War I is fought; the United States enters the war in 1917.

1939–1945
World War II is fought; the United States enters the war in 1941.

2001
Terrorists attack the Pentagon and the World Trade Center on September 11.

Words to Know

abolitionist (ab-uh-LISH-uh-nist)—a person who works to outlaw slavery

capital (KAP-uh-tuhl)—the city where government is based

capitol (KAP-uh-tuhl)—a building where lawmakers meet

Civil Rights movement (SIV-il RITES MOOV-muhnt)—the actions by thousands of people in the mid-1900s to gain equal rights for all people

district (DISS-trikt)—an area or region

Emancipation Proclamation (i-man-si-PAY-shuhn prok-luh-MAY-shuhn)—Abraham Lincoln's order to free all slaves in Confederate-held land; the Emancipation Proclamation took effect on January 1, 1863.

home rule (HOME ROOL)—the ability of an area to vote for its own leaders

lobbyist (LAH-bee-ist)—someone who tries to influence a politician's vote

monument (MON-yuh-muhnt)—a statue or building that is meant to remind people of an event or a person

plateau (pla-TOH)—a raised area of flat land

To Learn More

Deady, Kathleen W. *The Lincoln Memorial.* National Landmarks. Mankato, Minn.: Bridgestone Books, 2002.

Johnston, Joyce. *Washington, D.C.* Hello U.S.A. Minneapolis: Lerner, 2003.

Marcovitz, Hal. *The Washington Monument.* American Symbols and Their Meanings. Philadelphia: Mason Crest, 2003.

Witteman, Barbara. *Dolley Madison: First Lady.* Let Freedom Ring. Mankato, Minn.: Bridgestone Books, 2003.

Internet Sites

Do you want to find out more about Washington, D.C.? Let FactHound, our fact-finding hound dog, do the research for you.

Here's how:
1) Visit **http://www.facthound.com**
2) Type in the **Book ID** number:
   0736822046
3) Click on **FETCH IT**.

FactHound will fetch Internet sites picked by our editors just for you!

Places to Write and Visit

The City Museum
801 K Street NW
Washington, D.C. 20001

DC Visitor Information Center
1300 Pennsylvania Avenue NW
The Ronald Reagan International Trade Center Building
Ground Floor
Washington, D.C. 20004

The Smithsonian
Smithsonian Information
Smithsonian Institution
P.O. Box 37012
SI Building, Room 153, MRC 010
Washington, D.C. 20013-7012

The United States Holocaust Memorial Museum
100 Raoul Wallenberg Place SW
Washington, D.C. 20024-2126

The White House
1600 Pennsylvania Avenue NW
Washington, D.C. 20500

People dress in cultural costumes during the Smithsonian Folk Art Festival. The Festival is held in late June and early July each year.

Index

Adams, John, 23–24
African Americans, 5, 22, 29, 45–48, 50
Alexandria, 6, 21
American Indians, 19
Anacostia, 50, 53
Anacostia River, 12

Banneker, Benjamin, 22
Brown, Chuck, 48

Calvert, Leonard, 19
cherry blossoms, 50
Civil Rights movement, 29–30
Civil War, 5, 26–27
climate, 16–17

demonstrations, 29–30, 37, 46
Douglass, Frederick, 50

economy, 39–43
Ellicott, Andrew, 22, 23
Ellington, Duke, 48, 49

flag, 55
Fort Stevens, 26
French and Indian War, 20

Georgetown, 6, 21, 43, 44, 48–49, 53
government
    city government, 6, 32, 33–35
    federal government, 6, 7, 20–21, 23–24, 26, 28, 31, 33, 35–37, 39–40, 41, 52

Hoban, James, 23
Hoover, Herbert, 29

Jefferson, Thomas, 23
Joint Chiefs of Staff, 40

Kennedy Center, 15, 52–53
King Jr., Martin Luther, 30, 31, 46

land regions, 9–12
L'Enfant, Pierre Charles, 21, 22–23
Library of Congress, 51
Lincoln, Abraham, 4, 5–6, 26
Lincoln Memorial, 4, 5–6, 17, 30, 31, 43
lobbyists, 40

Madison, Dolley, 24
Madison, James, 24
Million Man March, 46
music, 47–48, 53

National Arboretum, 51
National Mall, 6, 31, 43, 46
neighborhoods, 34, 48–50, 53

population, 7, 29, 45–46
Potomac River, 6, 7, 9, 10, 11, 12–14, 16, 19, 21, 53
President's House. See White House

Revolutionary War, 20, 37

Rock Creek Park, 15–16, 53

seal, 55
security, 30–31, 42
service industries, 39, 41–42
Shepherd, Alexander, 28
slavery, 5, 26–27
Smithsonian Institution, 43, 52, 53

Theodore Roosevelt Island, 14, 16, 53
think tanks, 41
tourism, 39, 42, 43

U.S. Capitol, 6, 11, 12, 25, 28, 38, 43, 46
U.S. Congress, 7, 20, 21, 24, 28, 33, 35–36, 37, 40, 41, 52
U.S. Supreme Court, 33, 39, 43

Vietnam Veterans Memorial, 43

War of 1812, 24, 25–26
Washington, George, 20, 21, 22, 23–24
Washington Monument, 6, 8, 28, 29, 43
White House, 23, 24, 25–26, 31, 40, 43
wildlife, 9, 14, 16
    great blue heron, 14, 16
Woodson, Carter G., 47